Viola Time Scales

pieces, puzzles, scales, and arpeggios

Kathy and David Blackwell

illustrations by Martin Remphry

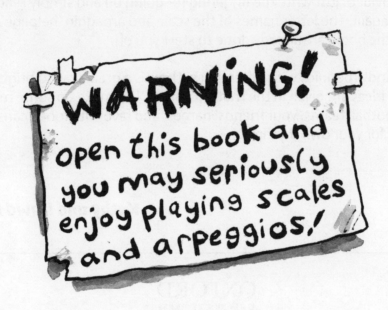

Welcome to **Viola Time Scales**. This book:

- provides two full pages for each scale and arpeggio
- sets out each form with a fingering chart, a telephone 'helpline' to reinforce the arpeggio fingering, and a rhythm game to practise the scale
- covers the finger patterns used in **Joggers** and **Runners**, beginning with D, G, and C majors, one octave, and moving forward to Eb major and D, G, and C minors
- includes a variety of fun pieces for each key and a range of puzzles and composition games.

MUSIC DEPARTMENT

OXFORD
UNIVERSITY PRESS

Dear **Viola Timer**,

Welcome to **Viola Time Scales**, where you'll find a lot more than just scales and arpeggios! Here are plenty of fun pieces to play, puzzles to enjoy, and chances to make up your own tunes.

Every two pages cover one scale and arpeggio. The fingering charts show you which finger pattern you'll need for each key. Have a pencil ready to fill in the letter names of each scale, and remember to check the key signature in case any of the letters need a sharp # or a flat ♭ sign after them.

The tinted circles on the chart are for the notes of the arpeggio. To help learn your arpeggios from memory, write down the arpeggio fingering like a telephone number in the space provided. Just write the fingering for going up and simply read it backwards to come down again. The letter names of the scale and arpeggio 'helpline' for D major, the first key in the book, are already done to start you off.

Playing scales and arpeggios with different rhythms is a great way to brighten up your practice. Some ideas are given in the rhythm games, but make up some more patterns of your own. Football teams, your friends' names, and favourite foods can all be starting-points for your own rhythms.

Have fun!

Kathy and David Blackwell

OXFORD
UNIVERSITY PRESS

Great Clarendon Street, Oxford OX2 6DP, England
198 Madison Avenue, New York, NY10016 USA

Oxford is a registered trade mark of Oxford University Press
in the UK and in certain other countries

Music and text origination by
Barnes Music Engraving Ltd., East Sussex
Printed in Great Britain on acid-free paper by
Halstan & Co. Ltd., Amersham, Bucks.

Contents

(Use this grid to chart your progress by ticking each scale and arpeggio as you learn it.)

* These pieces can also be found in the same key in *Fiddle Time Scales 1*.

D MAJOR one octave

Scale

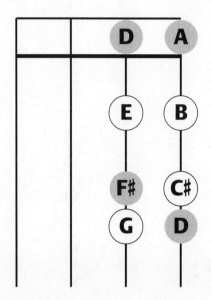

Arpeggio

Arpeggio Helpline: Ring **0 2 0 3**

Rhythm game

Play each note of the scale and arpeggio with this rhythm:

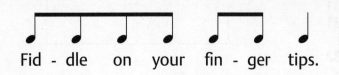

Fid - dle   on   your   fin - ger   tips.

Hold all fingers down – keep held down?

1. Finger tips

Try to keep your fingers down on the D string, and let your open A ring out loud and clear!

2. Low D, high D, A in between

Low D, high D, A in be-tween.

Low A, high A, low A a-gain.

Play the harmonics with a fast bow-stroke.

5

C MAJOR one octave

Scale

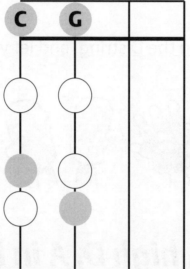

Arpeggio

Arpeggio Helpline: Ring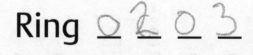

Rhythm game

Play each note of the scale and arpeggio with this rhythm:

Su – per   sprint – er

6

3. Super sprinter

Energetically

Try sprinting with the metronome! Start in the slow lane with level 1 and work up to Olympic standard.

Level 1: steady ♩ = 60
Level 2: in training ♩ = 80
Level 3: Olympic standard ♩ = 100

4. Step, skip, jump!

Rea-dy, stea-dy, step, and   rea-dy, stea-dy, skip, and   rea-dy, stea-dy jump: 3,

2,   1,   blast off!

*

Rea-dy, stea-dy, step, and   rea-dy, stea-dy, skip, and   rea-dy, stea-dy jump: 3,

2,   1,   blast off!   Blast   off!

* Complete these four bars by using the G string notes in the same pattern as the first four bars.

G MAJOR one octave

Scale

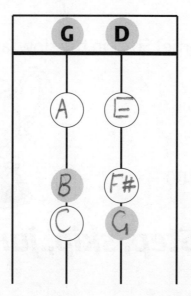

Arpeggio

Arpeggio Helpline: Ring 0 2 0 3

Rhythm game

Make up your own rhythm and play it on each note of the scale and arpeggio.
Write down your own rhythm here:

5. Follow me

I play first and then you'll fol-low me,— that's how we'll make har-mo-ny.

Hear the sound of this round, play to-ge-ther now and fol - low me.

This piece can also be played as a round, with an entry at the place marked *.

6. Ring my number

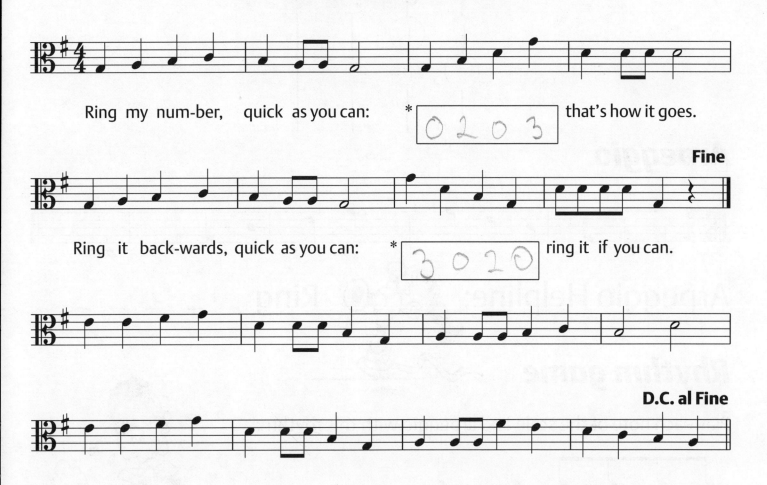

Ring my num-ber, quick as you can: * 0 2 0 3 that's how it goes.

Ring it back-wards, quick as you can: * 3 0 2 0 ring it if you can.

* Use the empty boxes to write in the fingers needed to play these notes.
Now try playing the first eight bars of this piece in the key of C or D major, starting on open C or D.

C MAJOR two octaves

Scale

Arpeggio

Arpeggio Helpline: Ring _ _ _ _ _ _

Rhythm game

Play each note of the scale and arpeggio with this rhythm:

Cus - tard   on   your   corn - flakes.

10

line: FACEG
paces GBDFA

7. Fast food

8. What's in your sandwich?

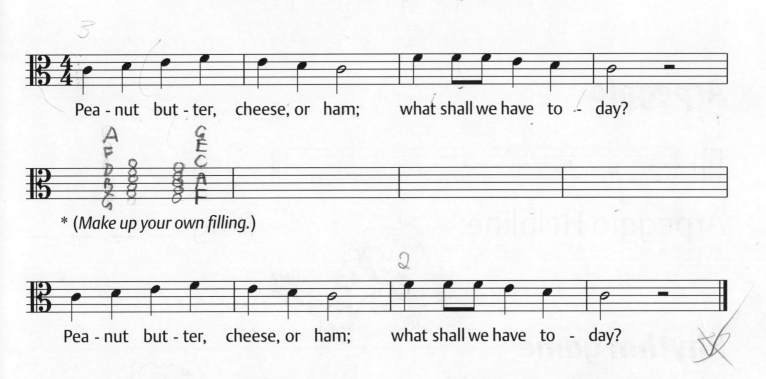

Pea - nut but - ter, cheese, or ham; what shall we have to - day?

* (*Make up your own filling.*)

Pea - nut but - ter, cheese, or ham; what shall we have to - day?

* Think of a foody rhythm and play it on the notes of the C major arpeggio.

11

F MAJOR one octave

Scale

squishy 2up

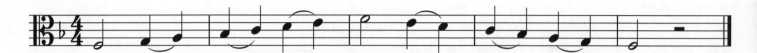

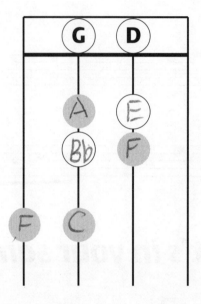

Arpeggio

Arpeggio Helpline:  Ring _ _ _ _

Rhythm game

Play each note of the scale and arpeggio with this rhythm:

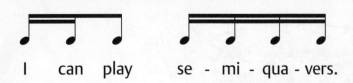

I   can   play   se - mi - qua - vers.

9. Accelerator

Steadily

mf

Slam the brakes!

3 short bows

cresc. longer bows

Be sure to start at a steady tempo.

Crash!

10. Double decker

Andante

mp

Fine

D.C. al Fine

Be a composer

Make up your own piece using some easy double stopping.
Try playing your open strings together, perhaps trying to sound like Scottish bagpipes!

D MAJOR two octaves

Scale

1st octave stretch 3rd finger
2nd octave normal finger pattern

Arpeggio

Arpeggio Helpline: HELP! Ring _ _ _ _ _ _ _

Rhythm game

Play each note of the scale and arpeggio with this rhythm:

Flo - ri - da   State

stretch 3rd finger - F# - _above_ stripe.

11. Sweet Betsy from Pike

American

When you can play this tune well, try playing it an octave higher starting with open D. ?!

- From memory
- Octave higher when confident by ear!

Be a composer

Find a rhythm that matches the words below and then write the answer in the empty box next to the word. The rhythms you need are scattered around the box. Remember that each part of the box is only worth one crotchet beat. Make up your own piece in D major using these American rhythms.

New York	
Maryland	
Pennsylvania	
New Jersey	

15

B♭ MAJOR one octave

Scale

Remember! This scale and arpeggio start with 2nd finger.

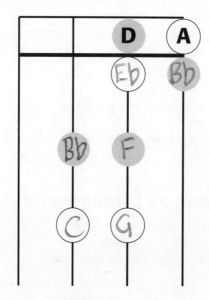

Arpeggio

Arpeggio Helpline:

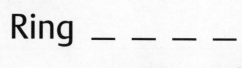

Ring _ _ _ _

Rhythm game

Play each note of the scale and arpeggio with this rhythm:

Two lit – tle an – gels.

12. Two little angels

Traditional

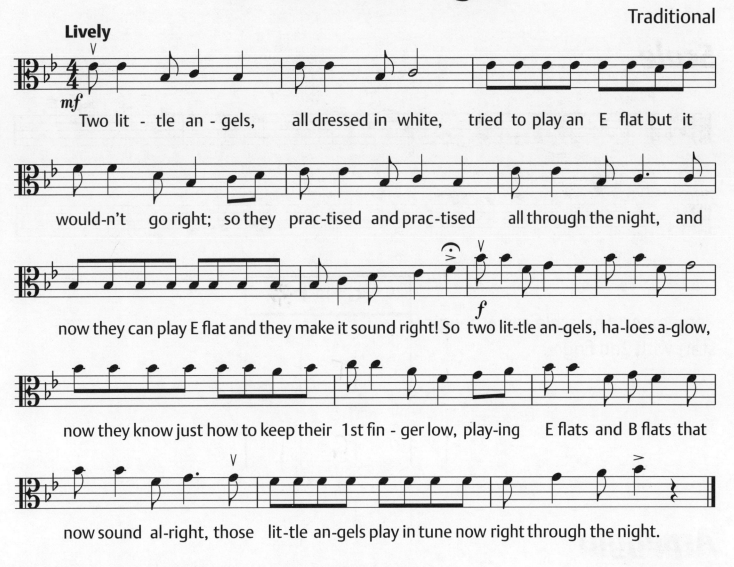

Lively

mf

Two lit - tle an - gels, all dressed in white, tried to play an E flat but it

would-n't go right; so they prac-tised and prac-tised all through the night, and

f

now they can play E flat and they make it sound right! So two lit-tle an-gels, ha-loes a-glow,

now they know just how to keep their 1st fin - ger low, play-ing E flats and B flats that

now sound al-right, those lit-tle an-gels play in tune now right through the night.

Make sure your 1st finger is in tune before you start.

13. Knock, knock!

'Knock, knock.' 'Who's there?' 'An - drew.' 'An - drew who?'

*

'An - drew the cur-tains so I could-n't see if you were in!'

* Using notes from the key of B♭ major, write down an ending to this musical joke.

E♭ MAJOR two octaves

Scale

Remember! This scale and arpeggio start with 2nd finger.

Arpeggio

Arpeggio Helpline: Ring _ _ _ _ _ _

Rhythm game

Play each note of the scale and arpeggio with this rhythm:

Bon - jour, mes a - mis.

14. French folk song

Ear this!

Try to play 'Frère Jacques' in the key of E♭ major.
Here are the first few notes to start you off.

D HARMONIC MINOR one octave

Scale

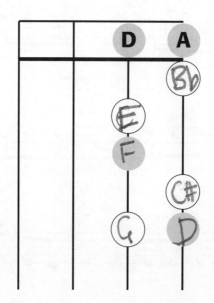

Arpeggio

Arpeggio Helpline:  Ring _ _ _ _

Rhythm game

Play each note of the scale and arpeggio with this rhythm:

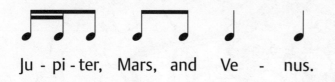

Ju - pi - ter, Mars, and Ve - nus.

15. Theme from Mahler's First Symphony

16. In orbit

Mysteriously

* Let your right arm 'orbit' in each of the rests.

Be a composer

Try to compose your own space piece. Perhaps your piece could tell a story. Explore your viola for some special effects: harmonics, *glissandi*, or playing with the wood of the bow are a few to try. Or take the rhythm of some space words and make up a piece using notes from D harmonic minor. For example:

Shoot-ing star

C HARMONIC MINOR one octave

Scale

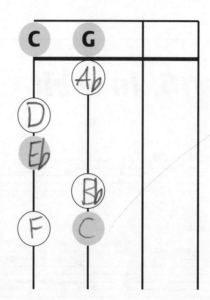

Arpeggio

Arpeggio Helpline: Ring _ _ _ _

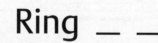

Rhythm game

Play each note of the scale and arpeggio with this rhythm:

C   min - or   is   the   key.

17. Old man of Peru

mf
There was an old man of Pe - ru___ who dreamt he was eat-ing his shoe.___ He

woke in the night in a ter-ri-ble fright! And found it was per-fect-ly true!

L.H. pizz.

Crack the code!

Work out what this says! The number '1' means find the letter name of the first note in the scale of C minor, '2' means the second note, and so on. Write the correct letter in its box.

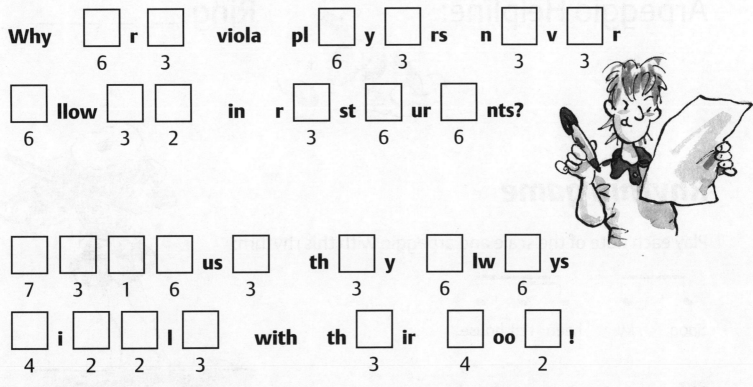

Why [ ]r[ ] viola pl[ ]y[ ]rs n[ ]v[ ]r
    6   3   6   3   3   3

[ ] llow [ ][ ] in r[ ]st[ ]ur[ ]nts?
6   3 2   3   6   6

[ ][ ][ ][ ] us[ ] th[ ]y [ ]lw[ ]ys
7 3 1 6   3   3   6   6

[ ]i[ ][ ]l[ ] with th[ ]ir [ ]oo[ ]!
4 2 2 3   3   4   2

23

G HARMONIC MINOR one octave

Scale

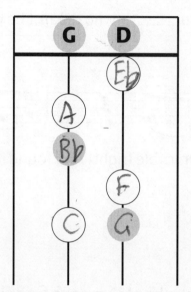

Arpeggio

Arpeggio Helpline: Ring _ _ _ _

Rhythm game

Play each note of the scale and arpeggio with this rhythm:

Spoo - ky   haun - ted house.

24

18. Haunted house

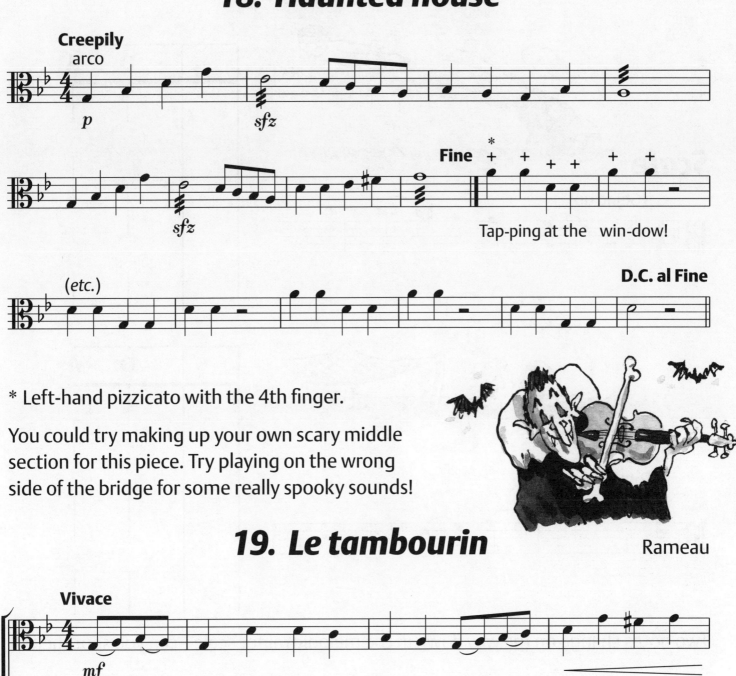

Creepily

Fine

Tap-ping at the win-dow!

D.C. al Fine

(etc.)

* Left-hand pizzicato with the 4th finger.

You could try making up your own scary middle
section for this piece. Try playing on the wrong
side of the bridge for some really spooky sounds!

19. Le tambourin

Rameau

Vivace

D MELODIC MINOR one octave

Scale

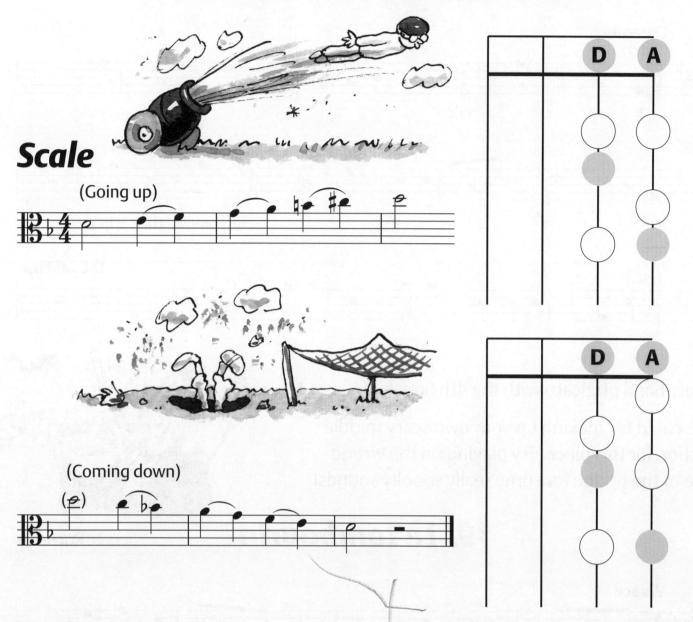

(Going up)

(Coming down)

Two notes change on the way down in the melodic minor scale—can you spot them?

Arpeggio

Look back to page 20 for the notes of the D minor arpeggio.

Rhythm game

Play each note of the scale and arpeggio with this rhythm:

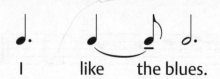

I   like   the blues.

20. I gotta play those viola blues

21. Shalom Chaverim

Israeli

This is a minor-key round. It can be played in three parts with an entry at each of the places marked *.

C MELODIC MINOR one octave

Scale

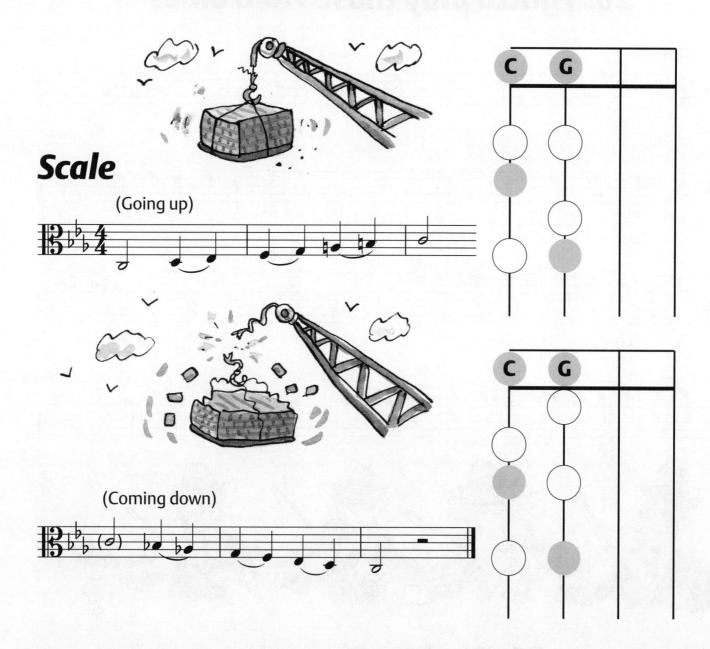

(Going up)

(Coming down)

Two notes change on the way down in the melodic minor scale—can you spot them?

Arpeggio

Look back to page 22 for the notes of the C minor arpeggio.

Rhythm game

Make up your own rhythm and play it on each note of the scale and arpeggio.
Write down your own rhythm here:

22. We walk a narrow way

Israeli

23. Escalator cha-cha

Fill in the missing notes. Add three crotchets to each incomplete bar. Use the ascending G string notes from C melodic minor when the escalator is going 'up' and the descending G string notes when the escalator is coming 'down'.

G MELODIC MINOR one octave

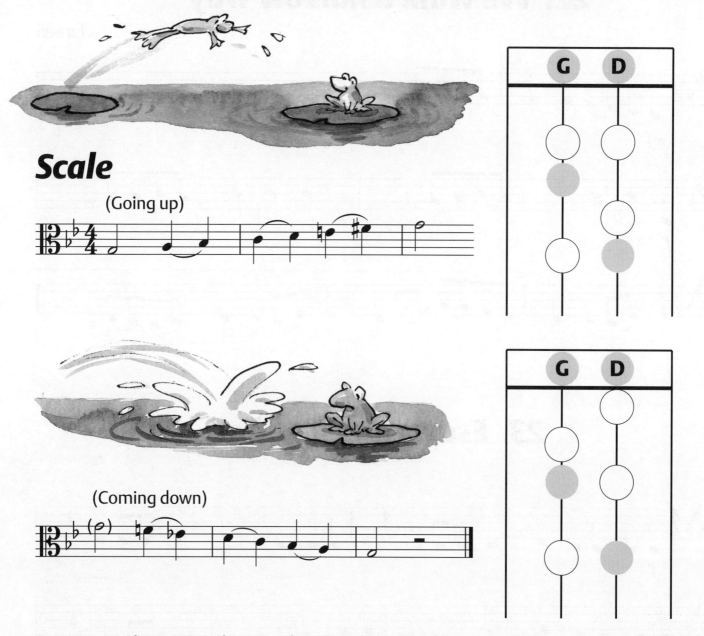

Scale

(Going up)

(Coming down)

Two notes change on the way down in the melodic minor scale—can you spot them?

Arpeggio

Look back to page 24 for the notes of the G minor arpeggio.

Rhythm game

Play each note of the scale and arpeggio with this rhythm:

F   sharp   or   F   nat - 'ral?

24. A bit of Bach

J. S. Bach (adapted)

25. Mean street chase 2

A different version of this piece can be found in *Viola Time Runners* (p. 17).

Things to do with your scales and arpeggios

Play them **Loudly** *(f)*

PLAY A SCALE WITH SLURRED BOWING

Ear this!
Play 'Twinkle, twinkle' or 'London's burning'
in every major key in this book

Play your scales with
separate bows

Play them quietly (p)

Play them with different rhythms
—perhaps from your topic at school:

Queen Vic - to - ri - a, Prince   Al - bert

Play a **SPOOKY** scale using tremolo bowing

Play a scale
PIZZICATO

Find a friend and play them as rounds like this:

Scale

Arpeggio

etc.

SPRINT THROUGH YOUR BEST
SCALE AT HIGH SPEED!